YOU'RE THE CHEF

AWESOME Snacks AND Appetizers

Kari Cornell Photographs by **Brie Cohen**

M MILLBROOK PRESS • MINNEAPOLIS

For my mom, who taught me how to experiment in the kitchen; and for Will, Theo, and Brian, who cheerfully sampled every snack and appetizer I put on the table —K.C.

For Lerner production editors Sarah, Jen, Julie, Erica, Heidi, and Martha —B.C.

Photography by Brie Cohen
Food in photographs prepared by chef David Vlach
Illustrations by Laura Westlund/Independent Picture Service
The image on page 5 is used with the permission of © iStockphoto.com/stuartbur.

Allergy alert: The recipes in this book contain ingredients to which some people can be allergic. Anyone with food allergies or sensitivities should follow the advice of a physician or other medical professional.

Millbrook Press
A division of Lerner Publishing Group, Inc.
241 First Avenue North
Minneapolis, MN 55401 U.S.A.

Website address: www.lernerbooks.com

Main body text set in Felbridge Std Regular 11/14.
Typeface provided by Monotype Typography.

Library of Congress Cataloging-in-Publication Data

Cornell, Kari A.
Awesome snacks and appetizers / by Kari Cornell ; photographs by Brie Cohen.
pages   cm. — (You're the chef)
Includes index.
ISBN 978–0–7613–6642–3 (lib. bdg. : alk. paper)
ISBN 978–1–4677–1717–5 (eBook)
1. Snack foods—Juvenile literature. 2. Appetizers—Juvenile literature.
I. Cohen, Brie, photographer. II. Title.
TX740.C665 2014
642—dc23   2012048903

Manufactured in the United States of America
1 – CG – 7/15/13

TABLE OF CONTENTS

Are you ready to make some fun appetizers and party food?

YOU can be the chef and make food for yourself and your family. These easy recipes are perfect for a chef who is just learning to cook. And they're so delicious, you'll want to make them again and again!

I developed these recipes with the help of my kids, who are six and eight years old. They can't do all the cooking on their own yet, but they can do a lot.

Can't get enough of cooking? Check out www.lerneresource.com for bonus recipes, healthful eating tips, links to cooking technique videos, and more!

BEFORE YOU START

Reserve your space! Always ask for permission to work in the kitchen.

Find a helper! You will need an adult helper for some tasks. Talk with this person to decide what steps you can do on your own and what steps the adult will help with.

Make a plan! Read through the whole recipe before you start cooking. Do you have the ingredients you'll need? If you don't know what a certain ingredient is, see page 31 to find out more. Do you understand each step? If you don't understand a technique, such as *whisk* or *slice*, turn to page 7. At the beginning of each recipe, you'll see how much time you'll need to prepare the recipe and to cook it. The recipe will also tell you how many servings it makes. Small drawings at the top of each recipe let you know what major kitchen equipment you'll need—such as a stovetop, a food processor, or a microwave.

stovetop

food processor

knives

microwave

oven

Wash up! Always wash your hands with soap and water before you start cooking. And wash them again after you touch raw eggs, meat, or fish.

Get it together! Find the tools you'll use, such as measuring cups or a mixing bowl. Gather all the ingredients you'll need. That way you won't have to stop to look for things once you start cooking.

SAFETY TIPS

That's sharp! Your adult helper needs to be in the kitchen when you are using a knife, a grater, or a peeler. If you are doing the cutting, use a cutting board. Cut away from your body, and keep your fingers away from the blade.

That's hot! Be sure an adult is in the kitchen if you use the stove or the oven. Your adult helper can help you cook on the stove and take hot things out of the oven.

Tie it back! If you have long hair, tie it back or wear a hat. If you have long sleeves, roll them up. You want to keep your hair and clothing out of the food and away from flames or other heat sources.

Turn that handle! When cooking on the stove, turn the pot handle toward the back. That way, no one will accidentally bump the pot and knock it off the stove.

Wash it! If you are working with raw eggs or meat, you need to keep things extra clean. After cutting raw meat or fish, wash the knife and the cutting board right away. They must be clean before you use them to cut anything else.

Go slowly! Take your time when you're working. When you are doing something for the first time, such as peeling or grating, be sure not to rush.

Above all, have fun!

Finish the job right!

One of your most important jobs as a chef is to clean up when you're done. Wash the dishes with soap and warm water. Wipe off the countertop or the table. Put away any unused ingredients. The adults in your house will be more excited for you to cook next time if you take charge of cleaning up.

COOKING TOOLS

bowls

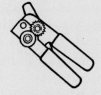

can opener

colander

cookie sheet

cutting board

dry measuring cups

fork

frying pan

knives

liquid measuring cup

measuring spoons

oven mitt

pastry brush

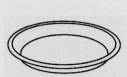

pie pan

pizza cutter

saucepans

serrated knife

skewers

slotted spoon

spatula

spoon

table knife

tongs

whisk

wooden spoon

TECHNIQUES

bake: to cook in the oven

boil: to heat liquid on a stovetop until the liquid starts to bubble

chop: to cut food into small pieces using a knife

cover: to put a lid on a pan or pot containing food

discard: to throw away or put in a compost bin. Discarded parts of fruits and vegetables and eggshells can be put in a compost bin, if you have one.

drain: to pour the liquid off a food. You can drain food by pouring it into a colander or a strainer. If you are draining water or juice from canned food, you can also use the lid to hold the food back while the liquid pours out.

fry: to cook in a pan, usually in oil or butter, until lightly browned and cooked through

grease: to rub butter or oil on a pan or in muffin tins to prevent food from sticking when it bakes

mix: to stir food using a spoon or a fork

preheat: to turn the oven to the temperature you will need for baking. An oven takes about 15 minutes to heat up.

set aside: to put nearby in a bowl or a plate or on a clean workspace

slice: to cut food into thin pieces

sprinkle: to scatter on top

whisk: to stir quickly with a fork or a whisk

MEASURING

To measure **dry ingredients**, such as sugar or flour, spoon the ingredient into a measuring cup until it is full. Then use the back of a table knife to level it off. Do not pack it down unless the recipe tells you to. Do not use measuring cups made for liquids.

When you're measuring a **liquid**, such as milk or water, use a clear glass or plastic measuring cup. Set the cup on the table or a counter and pour the liquid into the cup. Pour slowly and stop when the liquid has reached the correct line.

Don't measure your ingredients over the bowl they will go into. If you accidentally spill, you might have way too much!

serves 6 to 8

preparation time: 15 minutes
baking time: 12 to 14 minutes

ingredients:

2 8-ounce tubes crescent roll
    dough
1 8-ounce package (2 cups)
    shredded cheddar cheese
1 14-ounce package precooked
    cocktail hot dogs
ketchup and mustard

equipment:

measuring spoons
2 cookie sheets
oven mitts

Pigs in a Blanket

These bite-size hot dogs wrapped in dough
are fun and easy to make!

1. **Preheat** the oven to 350°F.

2. **Open** the cardboard crescent roll tubes
   according to the package instructions.

3. **Separate** the dough
   triangles and unroll each of
   them. **Place** the triangles
   in rows on a clean counter
   or table. Make sure the
   base of each triangle is
   positioned downward.

4. **Sprinkle** each triangle with 1 tablespoon of shredded
   cheddar cheese.

5. **Place** one hot dog on each
   dough triangle, about ¼ inch
   above the triangle's base.

6. Carefully **wrap** the base of the triangle up around the hot dog. Then roll up the rest of the triangle until the hot dog is completely encased in the dough. **Repeat** steps 4 to 6 to make each pig in a blanket.

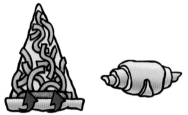

7. **Arrange** the "pigs" on two cookie sheets. **Place** them seam side down and 1 inch apart.

8. Use oven mitts to **place** the cookie sheets in the oven. **Bake** for 12 to 14 minutes, or until the dough is golden brown. Use oven mitts to **remove** the cookie sheets from the oven. Serve with ketchup and mustard on the side.

TRY THIS!

You can also make these with **veggie dogs**, cut into 2-inch lengths.

Leave out the cheese, if you prefer.

Add other condiments, such as **sweet pickle relish**, before baking.

Homemade Guacamole with Chips

Tasty and good for you, this green dip is great with your favorite tortilla chips. Or try it with the Black Bean Quesadillas recipe on page 16.

serves 4

preparation time: 15 minutes
cooking time: 0 minutes

ingredients:

1 large avocado
1 lime or small lemon
½ teaspoon minced garlic,
   from a jar
½ cup low-fat sour cream
1 tablespoon mayonnaise
½ teaspoon salt
½ teaspoon cumin
½ teaspoon chili powder

equipment:

cutting board
knife
shallow bowl
fork
small bowl
measuring cup—½ cup
measuring spoons

1. **Place** the avocado on a cutting board. Ask an adult to help you **cut** the avocado in half lengthwise around the pit. Use your hands to **split** the two sides apart. With your fingers or a fork, **pry** the pit from the avocado and discard it.

2. Pick up one of the halves of the avocado. Working over a shallow bowl, **slide** a fork between the avocado's skin and its green flesh. Run the fork all around the edge until the flesh is separated from the skin. **Scoop** the green insides into a bowl. Repeat with the second half.

3. Use the fork to **mash** the avocado into a smooth, thick paste.

4. On a cutting board, **cut** the lemon or lime in half. **Squeeze** one of the halves into a small bowl to get the juice out. You will need to scoop out the seeds with a small spoon. Repeat with the other half. **Pour** the juice over the avocado.

5. **Add** minced garlic, sour cream, mayonnaise, salt, cumin, and chili powder to the avocado mixture. **Mix** with a fork until combined. Enjoy with your favorite tortilla chips.

TRY THIS!

For extra flavor, add ¼ cup finely chopped **red onion** and 2 tablespoons of finely chopped **tomato** to the guacamole mixture.

You can also use plain, **low-fat yogurt** instead of sour cream.

serves 6 to 8 as a snack

preparation time: 35 minutes
baking time: 10 minutes

ingredients:

½ lemon or lime
1 small onion
2 tablespoons olive oil
1 tablespoon minced garlic, from a jar
2 tablespoons minced ginger, from a jar
   (be sure it's NOT pickled ginger)
1 bay leaf
½ teaspoon ground black pepper
½ teaspoon salt
1 teaspoon cumin
½ teaspoon coriander
½ teaspoon chili powder
½ teaspoon cinnamon
1 lb. lean ground beef
2 tablespoons plus ¼ cup canola oil
1 package egg roll wraps
1 jar of mango chutney
plain yogurt

equipment:

cutting board
knife
small bowl
small spoon
measuring cup—¼ cup
large frying pan
wooden spoon
medium bowl
2 cookie sheets
paper towel
small bowl
measuring spoons
pastry brush
oven mitts
spatula

Spicy Meat Samosas

Make these meat-filled treats as a snack—
or for a full meal. Serve with store-bought
chutney or plain yogurt. Yum!

1. **Preheat** the oven to 400°F.

2. On a cutting board, **cut**
the lemon or lime in
half. Set aside one of the
halves to use for another
time. **Squeeze** the
other half into a small
bowl to get the juice out.
You will need to scoop
out the seeds with a
small spoon. Set aside.

3. Using the cutting board and the knife, chop the
onion. **Cut** off both ends of the onion. Set the
onion on one of the flat parts you made by cutting
it. Cut the onion in half. **Peel** off and discard the
papery layers around the outside. Lay the onion
half flat on the cutting board. **Cut** the onion
crosswise into semicircular slices.
Then chop the slices into
small pieces. Repeat
with the other
half until you
have ¾ cup
chopped onion.
Set aside.

4. **Place** the frying pan on the stove, and add 2 tablespoons olive oil. Turn on the burner under the frying pan on medium and warm for 5 minutes.

5. **Add** the onions and the tablespoon of garlic, and fry for a couple of minutes. **Stir** often with a wooden spoon.

6. To the frying pan, **add** the minced ginger, bay leaf, black pepper, salt, cumin, coriander, chili powder, and cinnamon. **Fry** for one minute, stirring often.

Turn the page for more Spicy Meat Samosas

7. **Add** the ground beef to the frying pan. Use the spoon to break up and spread out the pieces so they are evenly distributed throughout the pan. Stir often, making sure the garlic and onions do not brown. **Cook** for about 7 minutes, or until the meat is cooked through and no longer pink. (If the meat looks pink, it is not done. Keep cooking until all the meat is brown.) **Remove** from heat.

8. Have an adult **drain** the grease from the pan. Transfer the cooked meat mixture to a medium bowl. Stir in the lemon juice.

9. **Grease** each cookie sheet with 1 tablespoon canola oil. You can use a paper towel to spread the oil around. Place the sheets next to you on a clean workspace. **Fill** a small bowl with a little water, and set it in your work area.

10. **Place** the first egg roll wrap flat on your workspace so that it looks like a diamond. **Put** a heaping tablespoon of the meat mixture on the egg roll wrap about 2 inches up from the bottom corner. Carefully spread the mixture in a 2-inch line across the wrap. Be sure to leave the two side corners empty.

11. **Fold** the bottom corner up over the line of meat to cover it. Then fold the left and right sides over the meat, as if you are making an envelope.

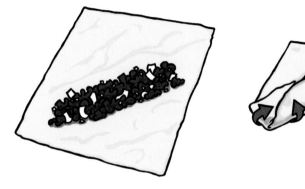

12. **Dab** your finger into the small bowl of water. Use it to **wet** the top corner of the egg roll wrap. **Roll** the entire samosa toward that dampened point. Press the damp corner down to seal the samosa shut. **Place** the samosa on the oiled cookie sheet with the sealed corner facing down. Repeat steps 10 to 12 until you've used all the egg roll wraps.

13. **Pour** ¼ cup canola oil into a small bowl. Dip a pastry brush into the bowl, and coat each samosa with a small amount of oil.

14. Using oven mitts, place the cookie sheets in the oven. **Bake** for 8 minutes. **Remove** the pan with oven mitts. Set it on the stovetop, and use a spatula to flip the samosas over. **Bake** for 2 more minutes, or until the samosas are golden brown. Use oven mitts to **remove** the cookie sheets. Cool for 5 minutes. Serve with the mango chutney and plain yogurt.

serves 6

preparation time: 15 minutes
cooking time: 20 minutes

ingredients:

½ cup canned refried black
   beans
4 large whole wheat tortillas
cooking spray
12 ounces (3 cups) shredded
   cheddar or Monterey Jack
   cheese
salsa or guacamole

equipment:

can opener
measuring cup—½ cup
wooden spoon
medium saucepan
large frying pan
spatula
cutting board
pizza cutter
serving plate

Black Bean Quesadillas with Salsa

Dip these yummy triangles into your favorite salsa.
Or try them with the Homemade Guacamole on page 10.

1. Use a can opener to **open** the beans. Measure the beans, and **scoop** them into a saucepan with a wooden spoon.

2. Turn the burner under the pan on medium. Stirring the beans, **cook** them until they are heated through. It should take about 7 minutes. Turn off the burner.

3. Lay two of the tortillas on a clean workspace. **Spread** ¼ cup of beans on each of the tortillas.

4. Spray a frying pan with a thin layer of cooking spray. Turn the burner under the frying pan on medium, and heat for 5 minutes. Then **place** one of the bean-covered tortillas in the frying pan, bean side up.

5. **Sprinkle** ⅓ cup cheese over the beans, and top with one of the plain tortillas.

6. **Cook** the tortilla for about 3 minutes, or until the underside is golden brown. (You can use a spatula to take a peek). Then use the spatula to **flip** the quesadilla. Cook until the second side is golden brown, about another 3 minutes. Repeat steps 4 through 6 to make the second quesadilla.

7. Use the spatula to move the quesadilla to a cutting board. Allow the quesadilla to cool for about 5 minutes. Use a pizza cutter to **cut** the quesadilla as you would cut a pizza. Serve with salsa or guacamole.

TRY THIS!

Add finely chopped **red onion** and chopped **red** or **green peppers** to the quesadillas when you add the cheese.

Make a tortilla pizza! Replace the beans with **pizza sauce**. Use **mozzarella cheese**. Sprinkle **turkey pepperoni** or other toppings on the cheese. Top with a plain tortilla, and follow instructions for cooking above.

serves 4

preparation time: 20 minutes
cooking time: 30 minutes

ingredients:

1 pound skinless, boneless chicken breast
½ cup whole wheat bread crumbs
¼ cup unbleached all-purpose flour
¼ teaspoon ground black pepper
½ teaspoon salt
¼ teaspoon paprika
¼ teaspoon garlic powder
2 tablespoons grated Parmesan cheese
1 large egg
¼ cup skim milk
3 tablespoons olive oil, plus more as needed
2 tablespoons yellow mustard
2 tablespoons honey
2 tablespoons plain yogurt

equipment:

paper towels
cutting board
knife
medium bowl
measuring cups—½ cup, ¼ cup
measuring spoons
pie pan or other shallow-sided bowl
fork
2 small mixing bowls
whisk
liquid measuring cup
large frying pan
serving plate
large slotted spoon
tongs
spoon

Chicken Dippers with Honey Mustard Sauce

These dippers are simple to make—and they taste great!

1. Take the chicken out of its package. Use a knife and a cutting board to cut the chicken into 1½-inch pieces. Transfer the pieces to a medium bowl and set aside.

2. In a pie pan, **combine** bread crumbs, flour, ground black pepper, salt, paprika, garlic powder, and grated Parmesan cheese. Use a fork to mix them together.

3. **Crack** the egg into a small mixing bowl, and **add** the milk. **Whisk** well with a wire whisk.

4. **Pour** the olive oil into a frying pan. Turn the burner under the frying pan on medium, and allow oil to warm for 5 minutes.

5. **Place** the ingredients next to the stove in the order they will be used: first the chicken, then the egg mixture, followed by the bread crumb mixture. Place 2 paper towels on top of a serving plate nearby.

Turn the page for more Chicken Dippers with Honey Mustard Sauce

6. Use a large slotted spoon to **place** 8 to 10 pieces of chicken into the egg mixture. **Stir** to coat each piece. Use the spoon to move the coated pieces to the bread crumb mixture. Stir carefully to make sure all sides of the chicken pieces are covered in crumbs.

7. Use tongs to **place** each piece of chicken into the hot frying pan. Make sure there's about an inch of space between each piece. Watch out for splattering oil!

8. **Fry** the chicken for 4 minutes on one side. **Flip** each piece over to fry the other side for another 4 minutes. Use the tongs to place each chicken piece on the serving plate with paper towels. (The towels will soak up the extra oil.)

9. **Repeat** steps 6 through 8 with the rest of the chicken. If needed, add another tablespoon of oil to the frying pan for each batch.

10. **Make** the honey mustard sauce. Measure honey, mustard, and yogurt into a small bowl, and mix with a spoon. Enjoy!

TRY THIS!

Instead of chicken, you can use extra firm **tofu** cut into 1-inch pieces.

No bread crumbs in the house? Use **whole wheat snack crackers** instead. Place one heaping cup of crackers in a blender or a food processor, and grind into a fine meal.

Add other spices to the flour mixture, like ½ teaspoon **thyme** or ½ teaspoon **sweet curry powder**.

Cheesy Fondue with Veggies, Fruits, and Bread

Fondue is fun at parties because guests get to take turns making their own snacks. Keep small plates close by to catch any drips!

1. **Wash** the apple, pear, cauliflower, and broccoli in cool water and pat dry.

Turn the page for more Cheesy Fondue with Veggies, Fruits, and Bread

serves: 4 to 6

preparation time: 25 minutes
cooking time: 7 minutes

ingredients:

1 apple
1 pear
1 small head cauliflower
2 stalks broccoli
1 loaf French bread
1 8-ounce package (2 cups) shredded extra sharp cheddar cheese
1 8-ounce package (2 cups) shredded Monterey Jack cheese
½ cup sparkling apple juice
¼ teaspoon nutmeg
¼ teaspoon paprika
⅛ teaspoon ground black pepper

equipment:

dish towel or paper towel
cutting board
knife
2 serving plates
measuring cup—½ cup
microwave-safe bowl
serrated knife
1 medium bowl
colander
medium saucepan
liquid measuring cup
wooden spoon
measuring spoons
1 package wooden skewers
4 to 6 small plates

21

2. Use a knife and a cutting board to cut the fruit and vegetables. To cut the apple, first **cut** it in half from top to bottom. Cut one of the halves in half again from top to bottom. Then cut out and discard the stem and the seeds. **Chop** into slices. Repeat with the second half. Arrange the slices on a serving plate.

3. **Cut** the pear the same way you cut the apple, and arrange on the same plate.

4. To cut the cauliflower, **cut** off stems and discard. Then cut the cauliflower tops lengthwise into bite-size pieces. **Chop** enough to measure 1½ cups. Arrange on a second serving plate.

5. To cut the broccoli, **cut** off the bottom of the stem and discard. Cut the rest of the stem into large circular chunks. Then cut the broccoli tops lengthwise into bite-size pieces. **Chop** enough to measure 1½ cups.

6. Place broccoli in a microwave-safe bowl with ¼ cup water. **Microwave** on high for 2 minutes, or until the broccoli is bright green but still firm. Ask an adult to **drain** the broccoli into a colander in the sink. Run the broccoli under cool water for about 30 seconds. Allow the broccoli to drain. Then add the pieces to the cauliflower plate.

7. On the cutting board, use a serrated knife to **cut** the bread into 1-inch-thick slices. Cut each of those slices in half. Place the bread pieces in a medium bowl.

8. In a saucepan, **combine** the extra sharp cheddar, Monterey Jack, and sparkling apple juice. Turn the burner under the saucepan on medium. Use a wooden spoon to stir the cheese mixture as it melts. When it is fully melted, turn off the burner.

9. **Add** nutmeg, paprika, and ground black pepper to the saucepan. **Stir** to combine.

10. Ask an adult to help you **pour** the cheese sauce into a microwave-safe bowl. Place the bowl on the table and serve immediately.

11. **Poke** the wooden skewers into veggies, fruit slices, or bread. **Dip** the food bites into the cheese. If the cheese cools and begins to thicken, heat in the microwave for 1 minute on high. Stir and continue dipping.

serves 4

preparation time: 15 minutes
cooking time: 20 minutes

ingredients:

6 large eggs
1 baby dill pickle
2 tablespoons low-fat
    mayonnaise
1 tablespoon plain low-fat
    yogurt
¼ teaspoon yellow or Dijon
    mustard
¼ teaspoon paprika
⅛ teaspoon salt
¼ teaspoon ground black
    pepper

equipment:

large saucepan with lid
cutting board
knife
large slotted spoon
medium mixing bowl
measuring spoons
fork
serving plate

Dilly Deviled Eggs

Make these delicious eggs with or without the pickles. They taste great for school lunch.

1. **Place** the eggs in a saucepan, and fill with cool water to cover the eggs.

2. Turn the burner under the saucepan on high. **Heat** until the water begins to boil. Then turn off the burner, cover the pan, and let sit for exactly 15 minutes.

3. While waiting for the eggs to cook, use a cutting board and a knife to cut the dill pickle. **Slice** it crosswise into very thin rounds. Then **chop** the rounds into very small pieces. Set aside.

4. When the eggs are done, use a slotted spoon to **remove** them from the pan. Place them in a mixing bowl, and fill the bowl with cold water.

5. When the eggs are cool enough to handle, **peel** them one at a time. First, gently knock an egg on a clean countertop. Turn the egg while knocking it until the entire surface of the egg is cracked. Start peeling the shell from the flatter end of the egg. You will see a thin, rubbery layer that covers the egg. **Pull** on this layer, and the shell will come off in large strips. Discard the eggshells. Repeat with the rest of the eggs.

Turn the page for more Dilly Deviled Eggs

Dilly Deviled Eggs continued

6. Empty and dry the mixing bowl. On the cutting board, **cut** each of the eggs in half. Pick up one of the egg halves, and turn it upside down over the mixing bowl. Gently **squeeze** the sides of the egg to remove the yolk. Repeat with each half, until all the yolks are removed. Set the empty white halves aside.

7. To the egg yolks, **add** mayonnaise, yogurt, mustard, paprika, salt, and ground black pepper.

8. **Mash** the yolks with the fork, and stir until the ingredients are combined. **Add** the chopped dill pickle. Stir again.

9. **Place** ½ tablespoon of the egg mixture into each egg half. Arrange eggs on a serving plate. If you'd like, **sprinkle** extra paprika over each egg for added color.

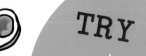

TRY THIS!

Leave out the pickles, if you prefer.

Sprinkle the top of each egg with ¼ teaspoon dried dill weed.

Apple Slice Sandwiches

Make these tangy, sweet snacks at home or while camping.
Choose your favorite toppings!

serves 4 to 6

preparation time: 15 minutes
cooking time: 0 minutes

ingredients:

4 medium apples
½ cup peanut butter or
4 ounces cream cheese
½ cup raisins, dried
cranberries, or dried cherries
½ cup granola
½ cup sweetened,
shredded coconut
½ cup chocolate chips
½ cup chopped walnuts,
pecans, or cashews

equipment:

cutting board
knife
1 paper towel
table knife
large serving plate
measuring cup—½ cup
5 small bowls

1. Use a knife and cutting board to **slice** an apple from top to bottom into ¼-inch rounds. Carefully **cut** the seeds and stems from the center slices. Repeat with the other apples. Then dab the apple slices with a paper towel.

2. Using a table knife, **spread** ½ tablespoon peanut butter or cream cheese on each slice. Place the slices in pairs on a large plate.

3. **Measure** the dried fruit, granola, coconut, chocolate chips, and nuts each into their own small bowls.

4. **Sprinkle** one apple slice in each pair with your choice of toppings from the small bowls.

5. **Place** a slice without toppings facedown on its pair with toppings. Repeat with all the pairs.

Crunchy Caramel Corn

I dare you to take only one bite of this tasty treat. It's so good, you can't help but reach for another handful!

serves 6 to 8

preparation time: 20 minutes
baking time: 1 hour

ingredients:

1 3.5-ounce bag plain
   microwave popcorn
1 tablespoon canola oil
1 cup brown sugar
½ cup light corn syrup
½ teaspoon salt
½ cup unsalted butter
½ teaspoon vanilla extract

equipment:

1 large paper grocery bag
2 cookie sheets
1 paper towel
measuring cup—½ cup
measuring spoons
medium saucepan
2 wooden spoons
oven mitts
waxed paper
large serving bowl

1. **Preheat** the oven to 250°F.

2. **Make** popcorn according to the instructions on the package. Let the popcorn cool a bit before opening the packet. (Watch out! The steam can be hot.)

3. Dry out the kitchen sink with a towel. **Pour** the popped corn into a paper grocery bag. Place the bag in the dry sink.

4. **Grease** two cookie sheets with canola oil. You can use a paper towel to spread the oil around.

5. **Put** brown sugar, corn syrup, salt, and butter into a medium saucepan. (Be sure to pack the brown sugar tightly into the measuring cup before adding.) Turn the burner under the saucepan on medium. Use a wooden spoon to **stir** until the ingredients are blended.

6. Bring the brown sugar mixture to a **boil**. Then set a timer for 5 minutes, and keep boiling the mixture. Have an adult **stir** it constantly so it doesn't burn.

7. After 5 minutes, turn off the heat. **Add** vanilla extract and stir to combine.

Turn the page for more Crunchy Caramel Corn

Crunchy Caramel Corn continued

8. Ask an adult to help you **pour** the caramel from the saucepan into the grocery bag of popcorn. In the bag, use a wooden spoon to **stir** as best you can. The popcorn should be coated as evenly as possible.

9. **Pour** the caramel-coated popcorn onto the cookie sheets. Use a clean wooden spoon to spread out the popcorn in an even layer. Use oven mitts to **place** both sheets in the oven. **Bake** for 15 minutes.

10. Use oven mitts to **remove** the cookie sheets from the oven. Use the wooden spoon to **stir** the popcorn on the cookie sheets. Put the popcorn back in the oven, and **bake** for 15 more minutes.

11. **Repeat** step 10 three more times (the popcorn will bake for a total of 1 hour). Use oven mitts to **remove** the cookie sheets from the oven. Tear off two sheets of waxed paper a little bigger than the cookie sheets. Place the waxed paper on a clean surface. Pour the caramel corn onto the waxed paper to cool.

12. To serve, **pour** cooled popcorn into a large bowl. Enjoy!

TRY THIS!

Add 1 cup salted cashews, almonds, peanuts, or pecans to the paper grocery bag after you add the popped corn. Or use 1 cup mixed nuts.

Air-popped corn or popcorn made in a kettle on the stove work great too. Have your parents help. Use 2/3 cup kernels and, if making on the stove, 1/4 cup canola oil.

In the fall, try mixing 1 cup candy corn or candy pumpkins into a bowl of cooled caramel corn.

SPECIAL INGREDIENTS

avocado: a large egg-shaped fruit with dark green bumpy or smooth skin, bright green flesh, and a large pit. Avocados are commonly used in dips and salads and can be found in the produce section of most grocery stores.

bay leaf: a dried leaf from the laurel tree used to flavor soups or meat dishes. Look for bay leaves in the dried spice and herb section of your local grocery store.

chutney: a flavorful dipping sauce or spread made from fruits or vegetables as well as vinegar, spices, and sugar. It is often served with Indian foods and may be found in the ethnic food aisle of most grocery stores.

cocktail hot dogs: bite-size hot dogs made from beef or pork that are used in many appetizers. Look for cocktail hot dogs at large grocery stores in the lunch meat or deli section.

coriander: a spice made from the seeds produced by the cilantro herb. This spice has a hint of orange flavor, and it is often used in curries. Ground coriander is available in the dried spice and herb section of your local grocery store.

crescent roll dough: a ready-made dough packaged in a cardboard tube. It can be found in the refrigerator section of your local grocery store.

cumin: a ground spice that is used to flavor many soups, Mexican or Indian dishes. Look for cumin in the dried spice and herb section of your local grocery store.

egg roll wraps: the outer skin of egg rolls. You can find egg roll wraps in many large grocery stores or in Asian grocery stores. Look in the produce section or the refrigerated section. If you can't find them, ask for help.

feta cheese: a white, crumbly Greek cheese that is made from goat's milk. Feta cheese can be bought as a chunk or in crumbles. It's available in the cheese or deli section of most large grocery stores.

garlic, minced: chopped garlic in a jar. Garlic in jars is in the produce section of most grocery stores. If pre-minced garlic isn't available, buy fresh garlic. Peel away the papery skin, and ask your parents to chop it for you.

ginger, minced: chopped ginger in a jar (not pickled). Although fresh gingerroot is available in the produce section at many grocery stores, you can save time by buying ginger that has already been minced. Look for minced ginger in jars in the Asian section of many grocery stores. Avoid pickled ginger, though, as this has a very different flavor.

FURTHER READING AND WEBSITES

ChooseMyPlate.gov
http://www.choosemyplate.gov/children
-over-five.html
Download coloring pages, play an interactive computer game, and get lots of nutrition information at this U.S. Department of Agriculture website.

Cleary, Brian P., Food Is CATegorical series, Minneapolis: Millbrook Press, 2011. This seven-book illustrated series offers a fun introduction to the food groups and other important health information.

Farmers Markets Search
http://apps.ams.usda.gov/FarmersMarkets/
Visit this site to find a farmers' market near you!

Nissenberg, Sandra, *The Everything Kids' Cookbook: From Mac 'n Cheese to Double Chocolate Chip Cookies—90 Recipes to Have Some Finger-Lickin' Fun,* Avon, MA: Adams Media, 2008.

This cookbook is a great source for recipes that kids love to make, including many snack and appetizer ideas.

Recipes
http://www.sproutonline.com/crafts-and
-recipes/recipes
Find more fun and easy recipes for kids at this site.

Snacks & Appetizers
http://spoonful.com/recipes/appetizers
-snacks
This website has many fun recipes written just for kids.

INDEX

You're the Chef
Metric Conversions

VOLUME

⅛ teaspoon	0.62 milliliters
¼ teaspoon	1.2 milliliters
½ teaspoon	2.5 milliliters
¾ teaspoon	3.7 milliliters
1 teaspoon	5 milliliters
½ tablespoon	7.4 milliliters
1 tablespoon	15 milliliters
⅛ cup	30 milliliters
¼ cup	59 milliliters
⅓ cup	79 milliliters
½ cup	118 milliliters
⅔ cup	158 milliliters
¾ cup	177 milliliters
1 cup	237 milliliters
2 quarts (8 cups)	1,893 milliliters
3 fluid ounces	89 milliliters
12 fluid ounces	355 milliliters
24 fluid ounces	710 milliliters

MASS (weight)

1 ounce	28 grams
3.4 ounces	96 grams
3.5 ounces	99 grams
4 ounces	113 grams
7 ounces	198 grams
8 ounces	227 grams
12 ounces	340 grams
14.5 ounces	411 grams
15 ounces	425 grams
15.25 ounces	432 grams
16 ounces (1 pound)	454 grams
17 ounces	482 grams
21 ounces	595 grams

TEMPERATURE

Fahrenheit	Celsius
170°	77°
185°	85°
250°	121°
325°	163°
350°	177°
375°	191°
400°	204°
425°	218°
450°	232°

LENGTH

¼ inch	0.6 centimeters
½ inch	1.27 centimeters
1 inch	2.5 centimeters
2 inches	5 centimeters
3 inches	7.6 centimeters
5 inches	13 centimeters
8 inches	20 centimeters
9 x 11 inches	23 x 28 centimeters
9 x 13 inches	23 x 33 centimeters